GSTAAD GLAM

Text by Geoffrey Moore

GSTAAD GLAM

ASSOULINE

INTRODUCTION

God once descended upon Earth and met with some soon-to-be Swiss farmers. He asked them what they desired, and without any hesitation, they replied, "Mountains and grass and cows, dear Lord, if possible, so we can produce milk, chocolate and cheese." So He granted their request and wished them the best of luck. Just as He was leaving, He asked, "The mountains will have snow and therefore you would develop ski resorts, correct?" They answered, "Yes, Almighty Father, we will build quite a few ski resorts, some of them large and some of them small." God answered, "I like the sound of a small ski resort, for it would be quaint and complement the traditional look of your soon-to-be Swiss-farm-life chalets. I like the idea of a village ski resort very much. In fact, 'Gstaadore' the sound of that." A witty response—a play on the French phrase *j'adore,* "I love."

The Saanen region in Switzerland was originally part of the county of Gruyère, which belonged to the house of Savoy. The area's core developed at the divide between the cantons of Valais and Vaud. The inhabitants traversed the alpine pass in the fourteenth century, carried by ox-drawn wagons, to arrive in

Graff diamonds are the accessory of choice on the slopes of Gstaad.

Gstaad. In 1402, St. Nicholas chapel was built, and the interior murals, from the second half of the fifteenth century, can still be appreciated today. The main occupations at the time were cattle farming and agriculture, but then came the great fire in 1898. Much of Gstaad was destroyed, and the town center burned to the ground. Local families came together soon after to rebuild. Reconstruction moved forward with the growing tourism industry in mind.

The opening of the railway line from Montreux to Gstaad on December 20, 1904, was the long-awaited awakening of tourism in Gstaad. If it hadn't been for the Montreux Oberland Bernois railroad, making its way through the Saanenland, the construction of ski runs in 1905 probably would not have happened, and the Gstaad we know today would be a different place. The establishment of the Gstaad Palace hotel and the winter campus of the prestigious Institut Le Rosey, both in the early twentieth century, put Gstaad on the jet-set map, garnering attention and continually luring people to the quaint town.

The residents, hoteliers, shopkeepers and tourist offices supported the construction of ice rinks, tennis courts, swimming pools, ski jumps, and ski and hiking areas to promote Gstaad and entice international travelers. The first ski school opened in 1923 and the first ski lifts in 1934, which were quickly followed by gondolas and chair lifts. During the World Wars and the Great Depression, tourism suffered greatly, and many hotels were unable to recover. A number of smaller accommodations such as chalets, apartments and private residences replaced the large hotels. In the 1960s, after years of improvements and new construction, Gstaad was dubbed "the Place" by *Time* magazine, having become famous for its part-time residents and vacationers who recognized its appeal.

My family first descended upon Gstaad in the sixties, at the behest of my father, actor Roger Moore, and much as the town has been developed throughout the years, it has always maintained its postcard image and feel. For foreigners, the first impression of the locals is that they're slightly cold, and the language barrier doesn't help the situation. But over the course of my time here, I have grown to understand their ways and traditions, and have seen a different side of them. Slowly but surely, they have opened their arms with respect and admiration.

During the seventies, the likes of Richard Burton and Elizabeth Taylor, Peter Sellers and David Niven and Dame Julie Andrews, arrived in Gstaad. All had three things in common: They were British entertainers in a foreign land, they appreciated Gstaad for its discretion and they loved sharing a large "jar" together, or as they called it, "Getting piste again." A jar was simply a whiskey sour with lots of crushed ice. Other celebrities of that era included Gunter Sachs, Aga Khan, Robert Wagner and Curd Jürgens. Different from similar ski-resort towns like St. Moritz, Gstaad has less of the bling factor and prides itself on a more low-key atmosphere. Perhaps this is why the English rat pack built their winter homes here, enjoying the luxury comforts and a much-desired privacy. French singer Johnny Hallyday had a home in Gstaad for a short period, and I once saw him working out at the gym in a leather jacket—I guess they don't call it rock and roll for nothing. Princess Grace of Monaco would come to ski with her children and her husband, Prince Rainier, who attended the Institut Le Rosey in Gstaad along with the Shah of Iran.

The locals didn't know or just didn't care who these herds of celebrities were. The famous guests would mingle with the residents in the same restaurants without any judgment from one side of the table or snobbery on the other.

Following pages: Writer William F. Buckley Jr. and economist John Kenneth Galbraith on a skiing holiday.

GSTAAD
GSTAAD 15
FANGLIFT
Attention
Attenzione
erwacht nur die
en und offenen Pisten
surveille seulement
e il servizio piste

On some occasions, I would tag along to Niven's house, where Taylor, Burton and Sellers were having dinner. They would reminisce about the past and their experiences in Hollywood, whether memories of the films they had made together or how the film industry was changing for the better.

Frank Sinatra and Sammy Davis Jr. came to Gstaad in the mid-eighties. One afternoon, we went for a stroll through town. As we made our way through the village, Sinatra turned and said, "You know, I have a black belt in shopping. Let's go for a spree, shall we?" We proceeded to enter one of the fashionable stores, and next thing you know, the shopkeeper fainted—a non-local, of course. Sinatra whispered, "You see, I told you I was a black belt in shopping. You didn't even see me strike a blow to his neck."

One year I was sitting in the salon of my family's chalet, and to my great surprise the Prince of Wales arrived unannounced. Dressed casually in a sweater, he asked my father if he would lend him a jacket for the evening. After finding the perfect fit, they went off to dinner at the legendary Chlösterli. A couple of years later, I had a similar experience with David Bowie, who showed up with actor John Hurt without warning, but unlike the prince, he came suited in a jacket. The restaurant that night was Sonnenhof, a simple establishment with red checkered tablecloths, and seated next to us was Tina Turner—the recipe for a magical night. The room came alive as they sang and danced.

The lovely Liza Minnelli and Olivia Newton-John also blessed us with their company in Gstaad, as did Christopher Walken and Grace Jones. Years later, John Travolta proposed to Kelly Preston in the lobby of the Palace hotel on New Year's Eve. One Christmas Eve was spent with Paul and Linda McCartney at their home in neighboring Lauenen—a holiday to remember!

Gstaad has an assortment of nice hotels to choose from, and most of them have a rich history. In April 1912, the construction of the Palace hotel began, the first luxury hotel in the region, and it officially opened its doors on December 8, 1913. The hotel, situated in the sought-after Oberbort neighborhood, houses La Fromagerie restaurant, which has had several iterations. During World War II, it held Switzerland's gold-bullion reserve, and after that, it was a bowling alley. The view from the Palace is spectacular, offering a unique perspective of the valley, and it always surprises me—no matter how many times I see it, I'm still taken aback. I remind myself every day of how lucky we all are to be living in this region. Perhaps that's why I chose to raise a family here. Both my daughters were born in Gstaad, so the love and respect they have for this small village is innate.

Hotel Olden and the Grand Bellevue hotel are in the heart of the village. The latter was built in 1912 as a cure house and spa. Then there is the Park Gstaad hotel, the Alpina hotel and the Posthotel Rössli (in the old stretch of the village), each of which has a unique charm. Sixty years ago, Micheline and Heini Matti bought the Bühler house at the bottom of the Eggli ski mountain—the ideal location for skiing —and converted it into the Hotel Arc-en-Ciel.

The climate in Gstaad is simply perfect. It never gets too cold or too warm. The benefit of Gstaad's altitude of 1,050 meters is that the winters aren't as cold as they are in St. Moritz and Aspen, whose altitudes are higher. The only disadvantage is that there may be less snow in the years to come.

But this isn't the case yet. Skiing is a tenet of life in Gstaad, a bedrock principle that dates to the early twentieth century. The Eagle Ski Club was founded in 1957, perched on top of the Wasserngrat, one of the three main mountains

Following pages: (left) The coat of arms of the municipality for Saanen, depicting a crane, is a variation on the coat of arms for Gruyères. *(right)* Swiss Yodeling Festival in Gstaad, 2009, celebrating a time-honored tradition of the Swiss Alps.

in Gstaad, the others being the Eggli and the Wispile. The Eagle used to be a summer farm owned by the Matti family and was eventually transformed into the swanky, exclusive spot it is today. It was the second club of its kind in Switzerland, after the Corviglia club in St. Moritz.

Recently another ski club, the beautiful Club de Luge, opened on the Eggli and is comprised of two terraces: The upper deck is strictly reserved for members, and the lower is for non-members who wish to dine and enjoy the marvelous view. The Glacier 3000 resort has numerous pistes and free ride areas with views across the Alps, and at three thousand meters, snow is guaranteed almost year-round.

Some say Gstaad isn't known for excellent pistes. On the plus side, this keeps the crowds at bay. What Gstaad does have is terrific heli-skiing. In fact, it's possible to take up to seven runs on a given day—that is, of course, if you managed to slip away after dinner the night before to avoid the pulsating music of the GreenGo nightclub.

Skiing is not the only winter activity in Gstaad. Others include curling, indoor tennis, horseback riding, horse-drawn sleighs, husky sledding, cross-country skiing and ice climbing. The Glacier 3000 has a roller coaster and boasts a Mario Botta–designed mountain station. In the summer, mountain biking becomes so popular that the local bike stores are often sold out. The Golfclub Gstaad-Saanenland, in Saanenmöser, is said to be a nice challenge. River rafting, paragliding and hot-air-balloon rides are also a possibility.

Then there is the Swiss Open, in which I saw the beloved Roger Federer play one year. It was probably the busiest tennis open I had ever witnessed in Gstaad.

Throughout the years, many top players have competed in the tournament. The first edition was held in 1915 at the Gstaad Palace hotel in collaboration with the Lawn Tennis Club, but it's now a stop on the ATP Tour—and the highest-altitude venue for ATP Tour events in Europe. Gstaad also hosts the annual Hublot Polo Gold Cup, which has drawn many championship teams.

The celebrity presence in Gstaad has not dwindled in recent years. My family and I had the pleasure of meeting Anne Hathaway when she was staying with Valentino at his mountain retreat, called Chalet Gifferhorn, and it just so happened to be the year she won an Oscar for her performance in *Les Misèrables*. She even sang "Happy Birthday" to my elder daughter, Ambra. At the same time, Madonna was house hunting in town and was even close to becoming our new neighbor, until the Theodoracopulos family purchased the chalet first. The Theodoracopuloses are certainly not new to this area and, in fact, are considered veterans here, not to mention wonderful neighbors.

Because of its great quality of life, Gstaad has attracted more and more people. There was once an off-season, but no longer, and the demand for property can be overwhelming.

The chalets are all fairly similar, with a design influenced by the founding farmers who had promised the good Lord to keep the area quaint and rustic. The angles of the roofs are not only dramatic but practical, meant to withstand the heavy snowfall. Architecture firms such as Chaletbau Matti, Hauswirth Architekten and Rieder Architektur have been instrumental in constructing the Gstaad of today. As for interior design, some of the best practitioners include Tara Bernerd, Alexandra de Pfyffer, Tino Zervudachi

Following pages: The snow-covered village of Gstaad.

and Federica Palacios, who have worked on some of the most fabulous chalets in the region. Rolf T. Schneider, a friend and the notary in Gstaad, is known for his ability to wave a magic wand to help interested chalet seekers buy their future homes.

There are quite a few mountain lodges for hire to host a variety of events, from a business lunch to birthday celebrations to dinner parties. Some are old farms converted for entertaining, with wooden tables and roaring fireplaces. Rustic-chic haystacks lined with blankets are the preferred seating choice, to enhance the mountain ambience. If the theme is authentic Swiss, then the menu must include fondues, whether cheese or meat.

Gstaad has appeal and beauty in abundance. That's not to say other ski resorts aren't as beautiful, but they all lack the historic charm at the heart of Gstaad. The canton of Bern has managed to retain its traditional design aesthetic despite the amount of development in recent years, due to the strict planning regulations implemented.

One noticeable change is the growth of high-end luxury brands that have opened on the Promenade, which has changed drastically since my schooldays in the seventies. Back then you could drive through it, but now it's pedestrianized. During Christmas, all walks of life stroll up and down under festive lights.

Alex Hank could be credited with stimulating the art scene in Gstaad alongside Maja Hoffmann and curator Olympia Scarry with Elevation 1049, a festival featuring site-specific work and performances in and around town. *Mirage Gstaad,* by Doug Aitken, created for the 2019 iteration, is a chalet clad entirely with mirrors, absorbing and reflecting the immense landscape in which it is situated. Throughout the years, the art world has begun to see Gstaad as more of a creative hub, with new galleries popping up.

As for the music scene, there is the Menuhin Festival, held in the summer since 1957 and founded by the violinist Yehudi Menuhin, who vacationed with his family here every summer. Famous performers who have come through Gstaad include Ella Fitzgerald, Louis Armstrong, Marlene Dietrich and Nile Rodgers. For two days each year, the biggest country-music names descend for Country Night, never failing to draw fans.

Institut Le Rosey was a life-altering experience for both Gstaad and myself. Times have obviously changed since my early years at the school, but it was an amazing introduction and assimilation to the town. The Gudin family, who own Le Rosey, have done an outstanding job running it as well as preserving its traditions. The local bakery, where we used to buy doughnuts in the wee hours before class, was later transformed into a dinner-dance club situated on the path leading up to the Institut. You can imagine how many students frequented the bakery and then the restaurant.

From my time at the Institut, I remember walking back from the Wispile ski mountain and stopping at the local Molkerei to buy a delicious chocolate drink produced by the local farmers—it always hit the spot after a day of skiing. All the fresh dairy products from the Saanenland are wonderful, and one can become spoiled for choice. The local meats are exceptional, and depending on which region they come from, the taste is distinctive, recognizable. Ordering a cheese or meat fondue for lunch with all the finishings is essential, as is a glass or two of white wine to accompany the cheese.

Following pages: Valentino's mountain retreat, Chalet Gifferhorn, overlooks the marvelous natural landscape of Gstaad.

The Hotel Olden restaurant, run by Massimo Nava and his terrific brigade, offers great service and a dining experience reminiscent of Gstaad in the old days—simple elegance. The hotel's co-owner Bernie Ecclestone is a regular, and despite the assumption of bias, his preference remains steadfast. Perhaps it is one of the reasons he purchased the hotel in the first place. The most coveted table at the Olden restaurant is to the left of the entrance in the main room, where the likes of Edwards and Andrews, and Burton and Taylor, would always be seated. The restaurant downstairs, La Cave, was established by Fausto Donizetti in 1960 alongside his wife, Hedi Müllener Donizetti, an accomplished yodeler and daughter of the hotel's previous owners. La Cave featured a live band in contrast to the tinkling piano that played upstairs. At that time, when you entered the hotel, to the left was the *stübli* (lounge), popular with the locals for drinking beer out of a boot-shaped glass; they would caress their drinks as they fondly gazed at the fur coats whisking by the door.

The Sonnenhof restaurant is considered one of the best in the region. The veal Zurichoise is delicious, cooked with butter and served with a cream mushroom sauce and *rösti,* a pan-fried potato pancake. Sonnenhof's *rösti* is distinct for its use of small potatoes, peeled and grated, which give the dish more of a crunch. The view from the terrace is stunning and highly recommended for an alfresco lunch on a sunny day. Meanwhile, in the setting of a three-hundred-year-old former bell foundry, Nik and Simon Buchs serve a varying menu to crowds of locals at 16 Art Bar Restaurant in Saanen.

The Wildhorn restaurant in Lauenen used to include a unique show with dinner. The owner, Freddie, would perform his Elvis impersonation, singing on tops of tables with his guitar. Despite his heavy Swiss accent, which shattered the illusion, it was quite entertaining.

Chlösterli, on the outskirts of Gstaad, was run and owned by Rudy Müllener. Once upon a time it was a bed-and-breakfast catering to traveling monks who would rest for the night before continuing their pilgrimage. My father had his usual table there, which was a concealed booth and apparently now bears his name, despite the changes in ownership.

The film *The Return of the Pink Panther* was released in 1975. The creator of the franchise, Blake Edwards, had decided the movie would be shot on location in Gstaad at the Palace hotel, and more specifically at the hotel's nightclub, GreenGo. It was incredibly convenient for the director and the star (Peter Sellers), as they both had homes in Gstaad. The indoor pool featured in a scene when Inspector Clouseau falls backward fully dressed into the water. In those days a live band would play on a small stage where the DJ booth now stands. Today's music is diverse and welcomes a rotating schedule of top DJs throughout the season.

The air in Gstaad is rarefied, and every so often, when the southern winds blow, you can smell the sea. It is not uncommon to wake up in the morning and find fine sand blown in from the sub-Saharan plains. Geographically, Gstaad is far enough away from the madding crowds but close enough to get to any destination in Europe the very same day. Richard Burton once said, "No matter where we have to live and work, we only feel at home in Gstaad."

AAD   Burgers &
      Take away   033 744 74 44

"A beautiful house has to be in harmony with its surroundings. The village here is ravishing, without a wrong note."

Setsuko Klossowska de Rola, *painter*

66 Enchanting village in all seasons. Sound of cowbells in the summer, tranquility of snowfall in the winter.... The Palace overlooking the village, like a giant chess piece. 99

Homera Sahni, *producer of* In the Spirit of Gstaad

Fondues   Raclettes
Nature 32.-   Valais 34.-
Champagne & truffe 45.-   Etivaz 34.-
Safran 42.-   Gstaad 34.-
Cèpes 45.-   Brebis 34.-

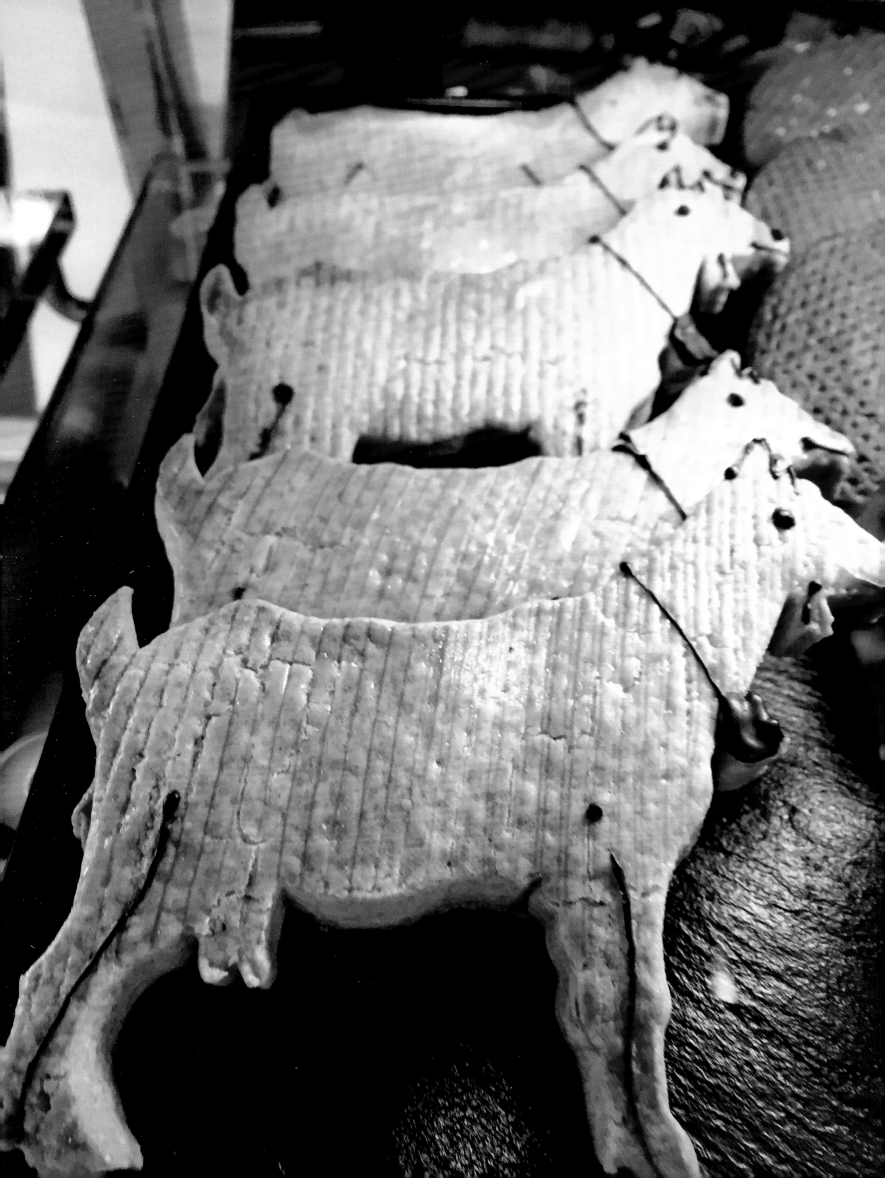

"It is the personal touch of the destination which guests and visitors enjoy the most. The entire world meets in Gstaad, in this tiny little alpine village. Furthermore, if you have ever arrived from Montreux by train you will wish to relive this magic experience over and over again. The wooden chalets, the cowbells, the farms and the barns…all this is a magnificently preserved authenticity."

Jean-Yves Blatt,
former general manager of the Park Gstaad hotel

"Every glorious tale you've heard about Gstaad Palace is true. I've always been with a merry band of troublemakers who makes sure every night is a night to remember."

Waris Ahluwalia, *designer*

"Gstaad is the name rather lazily used to cover an area about twenty-five miles square. The town itself ambles along a valley at three thousand feet of elevation. The towns…compose, loosely speaking, 'Gstaad.' And there is not a more enchanting area of that size in the world, we who go there say and think, swear to God."

William F. Buckley Jr., *writer*

Ich nahm den Wanderstecken und reiste durch die Welt,
doch fand ich keinen Flecken, der mir so wohl gefällt.

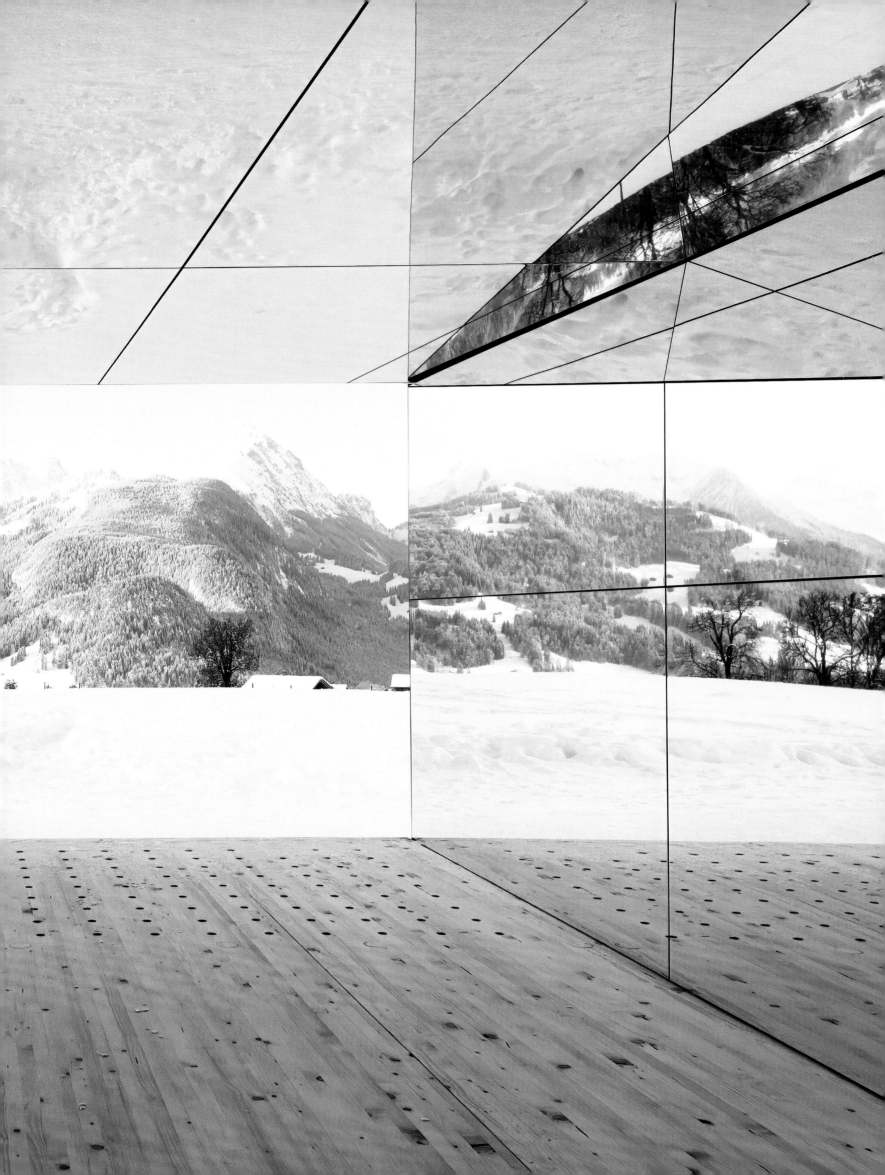

"Good-bye, Gstaad! Good-bye, fresh faces, cold sweet flowers, flakes in the darkness. Good-bye, Gstaad, good-bye!"

F. Scott Fitzgerald, *Tender Is the Night*

153

1 Princess Grace of Monaco with her children, 1961. 2 Skiers resting on the slopes. 3 Le Rosey ice hockey, 1960. 4 Snow biker. 5 Sabine Heller, then chief executive of A Small World, 2015. 6 Airborne snowboarder. 7 Actor Roger Moore and his family, 1993. 8 Ski race at Le Rosey. 9 Enjoying the snow in Gstaad. 10 Trumpeter Louis Armstrong with his wife, circa 1960. 11 The late decorator François Catroux at the home of Doris Brynner. 12 Racing driver Jackie Stewart, 1973. 13 Rolf Sachs and Princess Mafalda von Hessen. 14 Skijoring, circa 1950. 15 Eggli gondola. 16 Princess Bianca Hanau-Schaumburg, 1985.

Grüsse aus Gstaad

"Gstaad oozes glamour and style and is as picture-book pretty as anywhere on Earth."

Elizabeth Hurley, *actress*

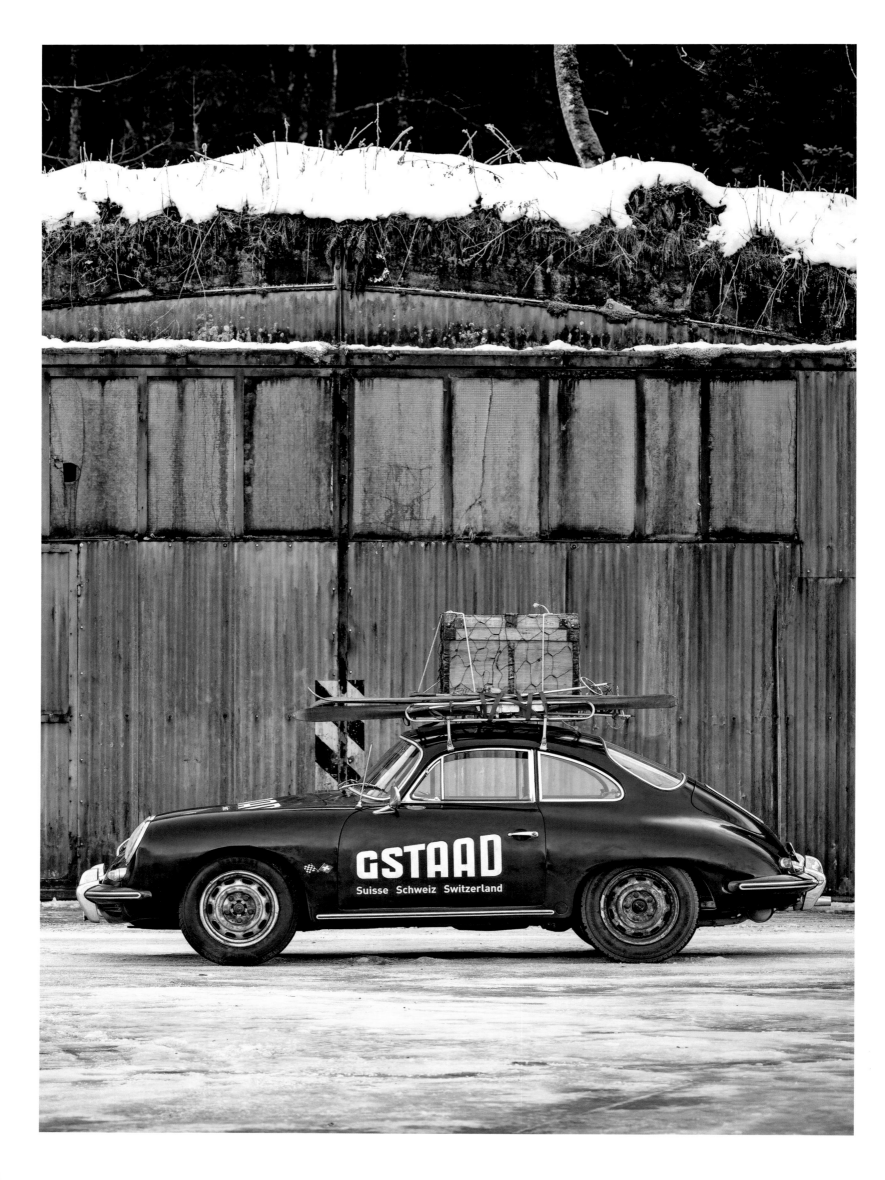

"Snow was falling, an oompah band was playing and hardy, wrinkled old men in lederhosen were smoking large curved pipes. Yet this was 1958, the country was Switzerland and it was for real."

Taki, *journalist*

"Planning to stay a month, I stayed a year—one of the best in my life."

Alistair Horne, *journalist*

66 Even as a child I came here to ski with my family. We have a very close and emotional connection to this area, which is why I am always so happy to come here when I can. **99**

Prince Albert of Monaco

1 Iglu-Dorf Gstaad. 2 Victoria Brynner and Frank Sinatra. 3 Luisa Moore and Sammy Davis Jr. at the Gstaad Palace hotel. 4 Mark Ronson and Joséphine de La Baume. 5 New Year's Eve party at the Gstaad Palace hotel, 1961. 6 Lauren Santo Domingo in Rougemont, 2014. 7 Photographer Rian Davidson (*left*) and Jan Luescher, CEO of A Small World, at the Gstaad Palace hotel. 8 Louis Armstrong at the Gstaad Palace hotel, circa 1960. 9 A pianist and a violinist at the Menuhin Festival. 10 GreenGo nightclub at the Gstaad Palace hotel. 11 DJ Tanja La Croix at GreenGo nightclub. 12 Bartenders at Huus Hotel. 13 A live music performance. 14 Elizabeth Taylor and Valentino, circa 1987. 15 A scene from *The Return of the Pink Panther* (1975), directed by Blake Edwards.

Olden

Parkieren verboten

"Never mind the insufferable jet set. Gstaad's great charm is its gemütlich style and atmosphere."

Mandolyna Theodoracopulos,
interior designer

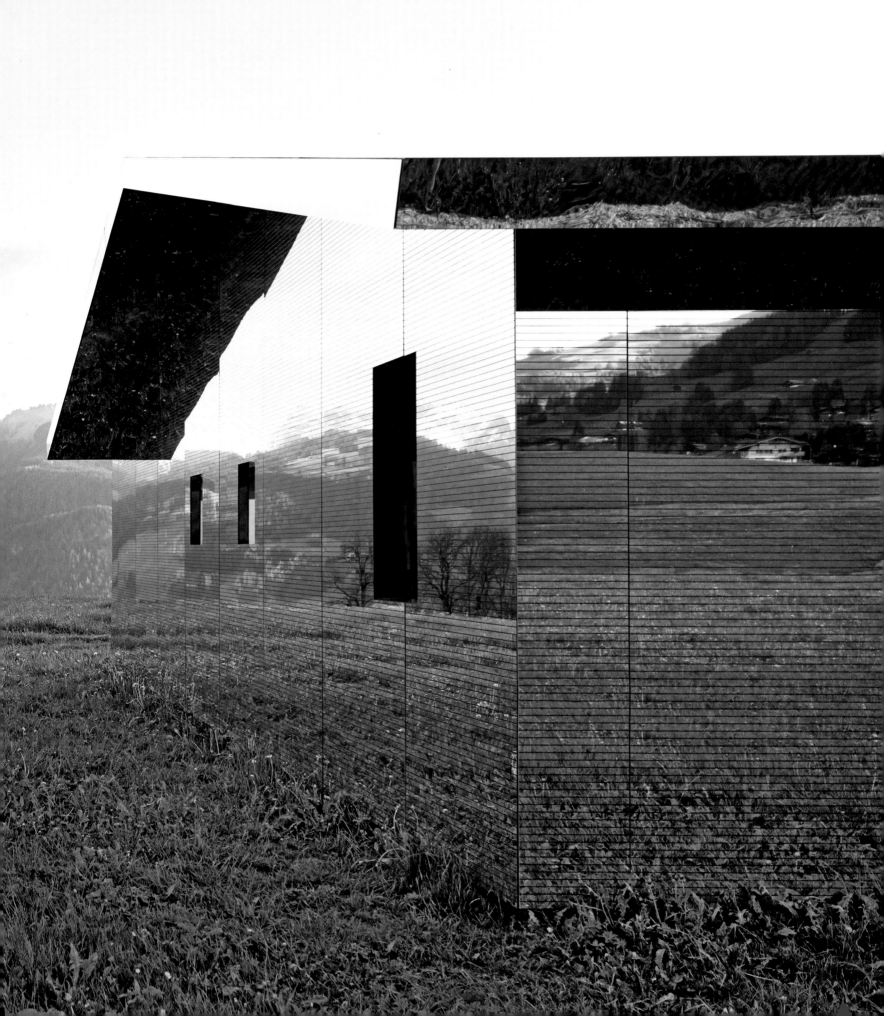

"It is the sheer, perhaps rather low-key beauty that keeps dragging me back to Gstaad: the sun setting behind the rumpled contours of the Gummfluh and the Rublihorn; the mist freezing on the willows along the River Saanen; the sharp wooden spires of Gsteig and Saanen churches; the sun-drenched plateau of Saanenmöser, with the MOB tooting in the distance; the Christmas fairy lights of Gstaad, and the Rougemont brass band playing in the courtyard of the Château."

Alistair Horne, *journalist*

" Here we have what most city dwellers don't have: the privilege of sleeping in a calm environment, breathing fresh air, hearing birds in the morning, smelling the rain and the fresh-cut hay, seeing wildflowers growing. **"**

Christian Hoefliger,
owner of Hotel Hornberg

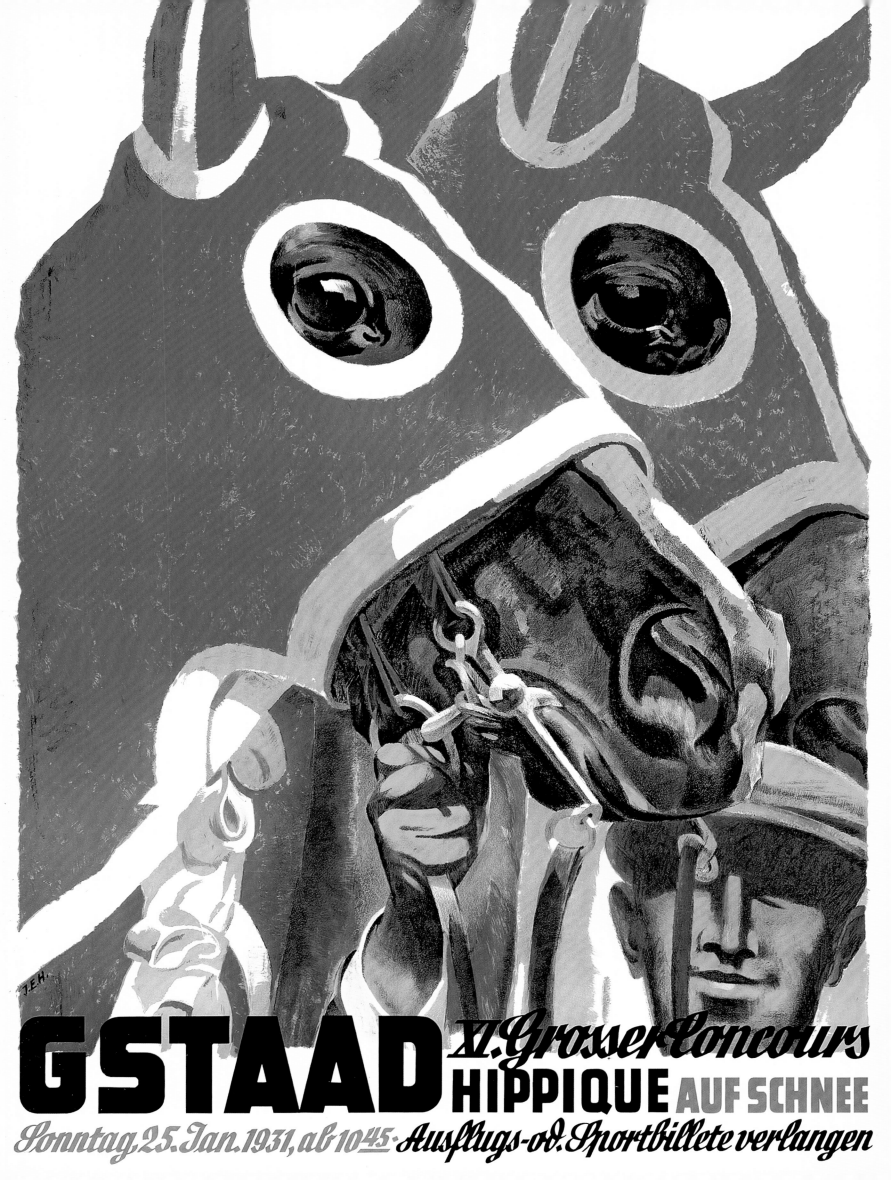

CAPTIONS

Guests having fun at the sixth annual Gstaad Winter Weekend Fondue lunch hosted by A Small World, 2015.

Left: Private jets are a favored method of arrival among Gstaad visitors.

Right: Five-star Alpina Gstaad in the Oberbort neighborhood, known for its sought-after properties.

Montreux Oberland Bernois railway traversing the countryside near Gstaad, circa 1930.

Left: GoldenPass Belle Époque train boasts romantic, retro-style cars. Trains are a preferred mode of transportation in Gstaad.

Right: Travelers at Gstaad Station, 1961.

Prince Alex Postiglione (*far right*) and guests attend A Small World Winter Weekend in Gstaad, 2012.

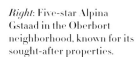

Horse-drawn carriage glides along Gstaad Promenade.

Shopping along the pedestrianized Gstaad Promenade.

Left: Brigitte Bardot taking in the sights of Gstaad, 1966.

Right: Classic cars line the streets of Gstaad, 1961.

Gstaad's charming architecture is safeguarded thanks to local building regulations.

Left: The village church of St. Theodul dates to 1453.

Right: Actress Anne Hathaway and designer Valentino take a stroll through Gstaad, 2012.

Reflection of a quaint village church in Saanenland.

Wally's Snack Bar proves that burgers and the alpine aesthetic are a great pairing.

Winthrop Rockefeller and his classmates take advantage of the fresh snow at Institut Le Rosey's winter campus in Gstaad, 1965.

Alfresco breakfast on the balcony of the Gstaad Palace hotel.

Le Grand Bellevue hotel is on Gstaad's chalet-lined main street.

Left: Model Nastya Belochkina photographed by Esther Haase for *Petra* magazine at the Gstaad Palace hotel, 2015.

Right: Students of the prestigious Institut Le Rosey in Gstaad, 1971.

Formerly the Pinte inn, Hotel Olden was erected following the great fire of 1898.

Left: Le Cerf, in nearby Rougemont, was established in 1958 by Jakob Bach, a musician, sportsman and baker, and his wife, Alice, a shopkeeper and cook.

Right: A view of the Alps is standard in homes in the canton of Bern.

Artist Frederick Sands at work in Gstaad, 1957.

The spire of St. Joseph Church as seen from Ambassador France Majoie-Le Lous's chalet.

Left: Designer Themis Zouganeli on the terrace of her home, Chalet Waldheim, in Gstaad.

Right: Handcrafted Themis Z plates complement the organic table setting.

Horse-drawn sleigh rides are on offer at Huus Hotel in Gstaad.

Architect Antonie Bertherat-Kioes's holiday chalet in Gstaad was converted from a generator station.

Left: Sculptural display of stags' skulls decorates the wall of the chalet designed by Alexandra de Garidel-Thoron.

Right: Fur-lined benches complete the dining area of Chalet Lauenen.

Artworks by Jordi Alcaraz and Maru Oriol, along with a collection of vintage photographs from Gstaad, adorn a home decorated by Luis Bustamante.

Left: Vintage four-poster bed at the home of antiques dealer Caroline Freymond.

Right: Alpine design details.

Fornasetti Lux Gstaad chairs, designed in collaboration with interior decorator Anne Lux, add a touch of whimsy to an all-wood interior.

Opulent Russian design elements and painted frescoes decorate the living room at the Gstaad home of Ambassador France Majoie-Le Lous.

Left: Vibrant colors and intricate carvings abound in the chalet of designer Lorenz Bach, 2014.

Right: Sabine Heller, Amirah Kassem and Teresa Missoni are all smiles at A Small World Winter Weekend in Gstaad, 2013.

Collection of works on paper by Donald Judd in a home by Luis Bustamante.

An alpine-chic interior is not complete without a stunning view.

Model Nastya Belochkina among the many luxuries of the Gstaad Palace hotel, photographed by Esther Haase for *Petra* magazine, 2013.

Left: Teresa Missoni attends a lunch hosted by A Small World, 2012.

Right: Interior of Chalet Homer, blending contemporary art and mountain decor.

Left: Cozy, warm scene at Huus Hotel — ideal for après-ski.

Right: Fireside sitting area at Chalet Colombe.

Fondue, a Swiss classic and perfect after a day of skiing.

Actors Robert Wagner and Roger Moore with Doris Brynner in Gstaad.

Left: Renowned bakery Early Beck in Gstaad.

Right: Mountains as seen from a wooden balcony.

Left: Pedro Ferreira, co-director of Le Grand Chalet hotel, in its extensively stocked wine cellar.

Right: Chef Edgard Bovier's Champagne Fondue with black seasonal truffle at Le Cerf.

La Fromagerie at the Gstaad Palace hotel serves all the rich, tasty Swiss specialties that visitors crave.

Left: The Eagle Ski Club terrace.

Right: Gstaad cuisine is made from locally sourced ingredients, including meringues, *doppelrahm*, fondue and *viande sèchèe*. La Cave, Le Cerf and Chlösterli are all known for their elevated classics.

Left: Dairy farming is a mainstay of alpine culture.

Right: Treats from the Early Beck bakery.

Left: Paper cutting is a traditional craft still practiced in Switzerland.

Right: Regina Martin, president of the Swiss Association of Friends of Papercutting Art.

Panorama of the rooftops of Gstaad.

Left: There are multiple toboggan runs in the Gstaad area.

Right: Vintage travel poster for Gstaad, 1940.

Geoffrey Moore and
Anthony Peck in Gstaad.

Left: Terrace at the home of art
collector, and former Le Rosey
student, Francesca Thyssen-
Bornemisza, near Saanen.

Right: John-Taki
Theodoracopulos after skiing
in his birthday suit, 2016.

Left: Gstaad Palace hotel rising
above Gstaad Promenade.

Right: Benjamin Blatter, chief
concierge of the Alpina Gstaad
hotel, with a furry friend.

Model Nastya Belochkina
exiting the Gstaad Palace hotel's
Rolls-Royce Silver Wraith
for *Petra* magazine, 2015.

Left: Naomi Campbell and Edward
Enninful arriving in Gstaad.

Right: Helicopter soaring
above the snowcapped trees.

Terrace at the Restaurant
Sonnenhof, with the Alps
in the background.

Left: Casa Santushti, Saanenland
home of Onno and Alexa Poortier
and their cat Hermés.

Right: Grilled tomatoes from the
Argentinean restaurant Chubut
at the Park Gstaad hotel.

Gstaad-branded vintage
Porsche loaded with skis and
other winter essentials.

Left: Text carved into the
traditional wood façade of
Pien Aardenburg's chalet.

Right: Winter in Gstaad is a
time for playing in the snow,
skiing and relaxing by the fire.

Left: Colder weather does not
deter participation in outdoor
activities. Tara Sahni in the pool
at the Alpina Gstaad hotel.

Right: Ryan Laver hiking
in Saanen, 2021.

Mirage Gstaad, 2019, by
Doug Aitken, is made
of mirrored aluminum
composite, wood and steel.

Mirage Gstaad, by Doug Aitken,
is a truly adaptable artwork,
reflecting the changes in seasons.

The exhibition space Tarmak22,
established at the Gstaad airport,
offers wonderful views.

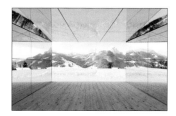

Artist Doug Aitken's *Mirage
Gstaad* features a house
covered with mirrors to allow
the viewers to navigate
a maze of reflective surfaces.

Skier painted by Louis Vaux, 1917.

Snow Drawing, by Olaf
Breuning, who used the Swiss
Alps as his canvas, 2014.

Left: Fornasetti Lux Gstaad panel, which features the face of the late opera singer Lina Cavalieri covered with a ski mask.

Right: Mountain restaurant Eggli overlooks the Porsche-designed cable cars.

The Wasserngrat is home to the Tiger Run, the steepest and most spectacular ski run in the Gstaad area.

Ski class at Le Rosey, 1970.

Left: Kobi Reichen, a professional mountain guide from the Bernese Oberland region.

Right: Snowshoeing in Saanenland.

James and Robert Redford skiing in Gstaad, 1977.

Left: Snow golf in Gstaad.

Right: Skier ready to make his descent.

Gstaad is a winter wonderland full of unique experiences.

Left: Jackie Kennedy in Gstaad, 1966.

Right: Gunter Sachs ready for the winter weather, circa 1970.

John F. Kennedy Jr. and his sister, Caroline, in Gstaad, 1975.

Left: Sir Roger Moore holding a sign in German that translates to "Greetings from Gstaad." The picture was a gift to his longtime ski instructor.

Right: Dining at a ski lodge in Gstaad, 1961. Photographed by Slim Aarons.

Taki Theodoracopulos, legendary long-term resident of Gstaad, and his wife, Alexandra, 2016.

Sled pulled by a herd of alpine ibex. Photographed by Reto Guntli and Agi Simoes for the Alpina Gstaad hotel.

Soaking up the sunshine on the slopes of Gstaad, 1961.

Left: The simple beauty of a snow-covered mountain is unmatched.

Right: Fashion company Letanne and social-media comedian Gstaad Guy collaborated on a collection of cashmere sweaters. Photographed by Joel Smedley.

Model Valerie van der Graaf and stylist Silja Lange at a fashion shoot in Gstaad, 2015.

An ad campaign for the Alpina Gstaad hotel, called "Beyond the Expected." Photographed by Reto Guntli and Agi Simoes.

Snow bikers conquering the steep slopes.

Left: Dogsled ride with huskies at the alpine resort Glacier 3000.

Right: Majestic reindeer in the Alps.

Iglu-Dorf Gstaad (Igloo Village Gstaad) in the mountains of Bernese Oberland.

Snow art decorates the interior of the igloo restaurant.

Left: Carriage leading guests at the Elevation 1049 exhibition, 2014. Photographed by Irene Kung.

Right: Kangana Ranaut at A Small World Winter Weekend in Gstaad, 2013.

Gunter Sachs and Mirja Larsson in a bobsled following their nuptials, 1969.

Vintage Porsche in Gstaad, photographed for the Christian Kohli Objects campaign.

Backyard at Chalet K in Gstaad, designed by Thierry Lemaire, featuring a white marble statue by Not Vital.

Balloons rise over snowcapped mountains at the Gstaad International Hot Air Balloon Festival, 1991.

Diamond heiress Carol Asscher, with artwork by Rob Wynne in the background.

Hockey on the frozen Lake Lauenen.

Left: Skis, ski poles and backpack—all set to hit the slopes!

Right: Tiger Run on the Wasserngrat.

Igloo built by guests at the Iglu-Dorf Gstaad (Igloo Village Gstaad).

Left: Opera singers Simone Kermes (*left*) and Vivica Genaux during the Menuhin Festival at St. Mauritius Church, Saanen.

Right: Fireworks erupting above the Park Gstaad hotel.

As nighttime descends on Gstaad, guests take to the bars and clubs for a bit of partying.

New Year's at the Gstaad Palace, circa 1960.

Left: GreenGo nightclub, the place to be since 1971.

Right: (*from left*) Adrien Brody, Sabine Heller and Waris Ahluwalia at A Small World Gstaad Winter Weekend gala, 2015.

The indoor pool at the Gstaad home of Carol Asscher includes a color-changing light feature.

Left: A photo from *The Rake* magazine of Alps & Meters alpine knitwear, shot at the Alpina Gstaad hotel.

Right: Huus Hotel bartender pouring a glass of Balvenie, a single-malt scotch whisky.

Left: Andrea and Tatiana Casiraghi at their wedding celebration in Gstaad, 2014.

Right: Gstaad aglow, with the Alpina Gstaad hotel in the distance.

Fiery sunset above the Wildhorn.

Greenery abounds during spring in Gstaad.

Gstaad train line from Montreux to Zweisimmen.

Left: Paragliding provides the ultimate view of Gstaad.

Right: Idyllic village of Les Diablerets.

Businessman Bernie Ecclestone's jet at the Saanen airfield.

Left: Purple and white edelweiss, a common flower found in the Alps.

Right: The Gstaad Palace hotel on a serene summer day.

Left: Saanenland has a close relationship with nature and farming.

Right: Windowsill of Hotel Olden highlights the alpine design typical of Gstaad chalets.

Players in the Hublot Polo Gold Cup ride through the streets of Gstaad.

Gstaad Promenade is rich with charming examples of Swiss-mountain architecture.

Group photo in Gstaad, 1964.

Mountain view from the executive penthouse at the Park Gstaad hotel.

Left: Susanne von Meiss lives on the upper floor of a chalet, originally built in 1782, which is located on an active farm.

Right: There is a cheese cellar in the basement of the chalet.

Swiss chalet style is characterized by widely projecting roofs and richly decorated façades.

Left: Luxury alpine clothing by Alps & Meters, photographed at the Alpina Gstaad hotel.

Right: Chalet White Ace is a private alpine retreat near the center of Gstaad.

Spotted Simmental cattle, the most common breed found in the Saanenland, drink from the trough on the Gstaad main street.

Left: Posthotel Rössli in Gstaad.

Right: The courtyard at Posthotel Rössli offers a relaxed atmosphere in the fresh alpine air.

Mirage Gstaad, by Doug Aitken, reflecting the beautiful greenery of the meadows.

Mountain bikers on their descent from Lake Seeberg.

Left: Musicians playing accordions in the fields of Gstaad.

Right: Perfect weather for a father-son hike through the Alps.

The authentic Swiss dish of cheese fondue is best enjoyed outdoors in the gorgeous landscape.

Alpenhornists on top of the Wasserngrat.

Left: Goats frolicking in the alpine meadows.

Right: Field of alpine white crocuses.

Victor Erdmann, Thomas Radmer, Mrs. Radmer and Gunter Sachs playing golf, circa 1980.

Untitled (1976), by Alexander Calder, displayed in Gstaad's dynamic landscape for the Hauser & Wirth exhibition "Calder in the Alps," 2016–17. Photographed by Jon Etter.

The Gstaad Palace hotel's Walig Hut offers a bucolic experience of Saanenland.

Chefs prepare for the Davidoff Saveurs Gstaad food festival.

Sounds of the Phly Boyz accompany a gourmet meal at the Wasserngrat Restaurant.

Horse and carriage ride through the countryside below a cloudless sky.

Farmhouse with geraniums in the Bernese Oberland region.

Audrey Hepburn in the garden of La Paisible, 1971, her home in Tolochenaz, Switzerland, a short drive from Gstaad, which she visited frequently.

Left: Hublot Polo Gold Cup, 2019.

Right: Mrs. Alfredo Cernadas reclines on a balcony in Gstaad, 1977. Photographed by Slim Aarons.

Saanen airfield is host to the spectacular Hublot Polo Gold Cup.

Summer activities in Gstaad include tennis, polo, rock climbing, volleyball and paragliding.

Left: Gstaad Polo Club logo.

Right: Vintage "Gstaad, Horse Race on Snow" poster by Iwan Edwin Hugentobler, 1931.

Hotel Olden seamlessly blends luxury with alpine charm.

Left: Wyclef Jean performs at the GreenGo nightclub for A Small World Winter Weekend in Gstaad, 2018.

Right: Luca Rubinacci, creative director of the Rubinacci clothing company, attends A Small World Foundation gala dinner, 2018.

ACKNOWLEDGMENTS

The publisher would like to specially thank Beatriz Aristimuno, Tara Bernerd, Doris Brynner, Homera Sahni, Mandolyna Theodoracopulos and Themis Zouganeli.

The publisher would also like to thank the following: Charlotte Jackson, Alamy Stock Photo; Maria Fernanda Pessaro, Artists Rights Society; Carol Asscher; John Warburton-Lee, AWL Images; Bergrestaurant Wasserngrat; Thomas Frei, Bernerhof Gstaad; Céline Bonnarde, Bestimage; Connor Norton, BFA; Stéphane Sésé, Boërl and Kroff; Nana Bottazzi; Levi Brand; Elizabeth Eames, Thomas Haggerty, Bridgeman Images; Hanna Büker; Calder Foundation; Elizabeth Kerr, Camera Press; Benjamin Pankhurst, Charlescannon; Cole Hill, Condé Nast Licensing; Rian Davidson; Luca Dotti; Jen Cox, Doug Aitken Workshop; Nusrat Epu Kazi Shaha, Epu Design; Baris Erdal; Leoni Marie Hübner, Esther Haase Photography; Pascal Zaugg, e621; Marie-Louise Emch, Faulhaber Marketing Services; Anthony Tran, Gallery Stock; Getty Images; Oberto Gili; Arnaud Magnin, Glacier 3000; Ella Dos Santos, Graff; Gstaad Guy; Markus Iseli, Gstaad Life; Eliane Zürcher, Gstaad Marketing; Christine von Siebenthal, Gstaad Menuhin Festival & Academy; Judith Schleifer, Kaspar Indermühle, Gstaad Palace; Raphaël Faux, Gstaad Photography; Reto Guntli; Simon Harris; Jennifer Voiglio, Hauser & Wirth Zürich; Nik Binggeli, Hotel Arc-en-ciel; Carole Stockalper, Hotel Le Grand Chalet; Ermes Elsener, Hotel Olden;

Annabelle Galley, Hublot; Craig McWhinnie, Joy Steinemann, HUUS Gstaad; Géraldine Pucken, Iglu-Dorf; Torvioll Jashari; Dominik Kauer; Faust Sabine, Keystone-SDA; Philippe Kliot; Irene Kung; Kim Lang; Laura Grohe, Laura Grohe Design; Ryan M. Laver; Le Cerf Rougemont; Le Grand Bellevue; Felipe Laurent, Le Rosey; Craig Shipman, LGA Management; Kelly Shaw, Lines+Angles; Sandra Roemermann, Luma Foundation; Martin Mägli; Regina Martin; Claire Menary; David Ratmoko, METRO Models; Ezzie Gladwell, Models 1; Nathalie Deppeler, Müller Marketing & Druck AG; Mark Nolan; Melanie Uhkötter, Nomadness; Fabrice Bielmann, Paragliding Gstaad Switzerland; François Grohens, Park Gstaad; Solina Mobèche, Polo Club Gstaad; Hanspeter Reichenbach, Reichenbach Architekten AG; Marcel Bach, Restaurant Chlösterli; Restaurant Rössli; Louise & Erich Baumer, Restaurant Sonnenhof; Gustavo Peruyera, Ricardo Labougle; Adrien Belanger, Road Works Management; Pascale Heuberger, Gisela Van Bulck, Rougemont Interiors; Rolf Sachs; Tara Sahni; Andrea Savini; Igor Schifris; Nina Repas, Oasis Watson, Select Model Management; Vincent Mounier, Shutterstock; Dawn Leikness, Splash News; Elizabeth Crespi, Tarmak22; Brenda Zimmermann, The Alpina Gstaad; The Eagle Club; Melina Vlachou, THEMIS • Z; John-Taki Theodoracopulos; Mariano Tribelhorn; Urs von Unger, Urs von Unger Gallery; Susanne von Meiss; Ruedi Hählen, Wanderverführer; Adam Whitehead; Alexander Williamson; Gabriele Bryant, YourGstaad; Vanessa Schwenter, 16 Art – Bar – Restaurant.

Assouline supports *One Tree Planted* in its commitment to create a more sustainable world through reforestation.

Front cover design © Martine Assouline.
Back cover tip-on (clockwise from top left):
© Urs von Unger Gallery; © Dominik Kauer;
© Prosper Assouline; © Irene Kung.
Endpages: © Melanie Uhkötter/Nomadness.ch.

© 2021 Assouline Publishing
3 Park Avenue, 27th floor
New York, NY 10016 USA
Tel: 212-989-6769 Fax: 212-647-0005
assouline.com

Printed in Italy by Grafiche Milani.
ISBN: 9781649800435